RAZORLIGHT

WISE PUBLICATIONS
part of The Music Sales Group
London / New York / Paris / Sydney / Copenhagen / Berlin / Madrid / Tokyo

Published by
Wise Publications
14-15 Berners Street, London, W1T 3LJ, UK.

Exclusive distributors:
Music Sales Limited
Distribution Centre, Newmarket Road, Bury St Edmunds, Suffolk, IP33 3YB, UK.

Music Sales Pty Limited
120 Rothschild Avenue, Rosebery, NSW 2018, Australia.

Order No. AM986689   ISBN 1-84609-691-X
This book © Copyright 2006 Wise Publications, a division of Music Sales Limited.

Edited by Tom Farncombe.
Music arranged by Matt Cowe and Arthur Dick.
Music processed by Paul Ewers Music Design.

Printed in the EU.

www.musicsales.com

Your Guarantee of Quality:
As publishers, we strive to produce every book to the highest commercial standards.

The music has been freshly engraved, and the book has been carefully designed
to minimise awkward page turns and to make playing from it a real pleasure.
Particular care has been given to specifying acid-free, neutral-sized paper
made from pulps which have not been elemental chlorine bleached.

This pulp is from farmed sustainable forests and was produced with
special regard for the environment.

Throughout, the printing and binding have been planned to ensure a sturdy,
attractive publication which should give years of enjoyment.

If your copy fails to meet our high standards, please inform us
and we will gladly replace it.

IN THE MORNING

Song by Johnny Borrell
Music by Razorlight

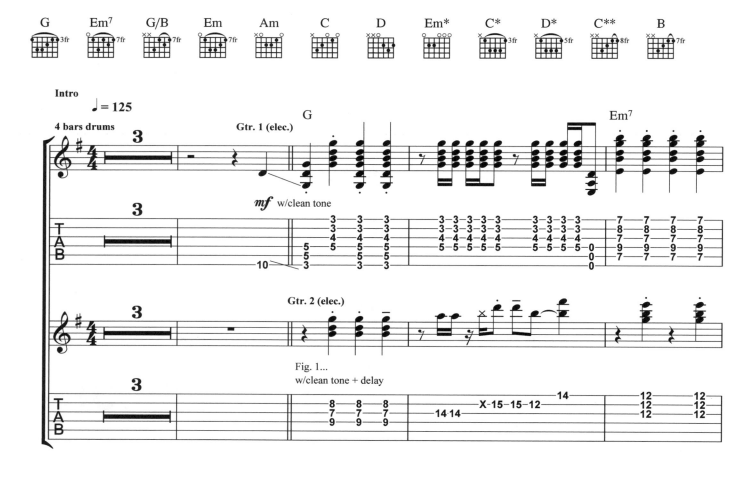

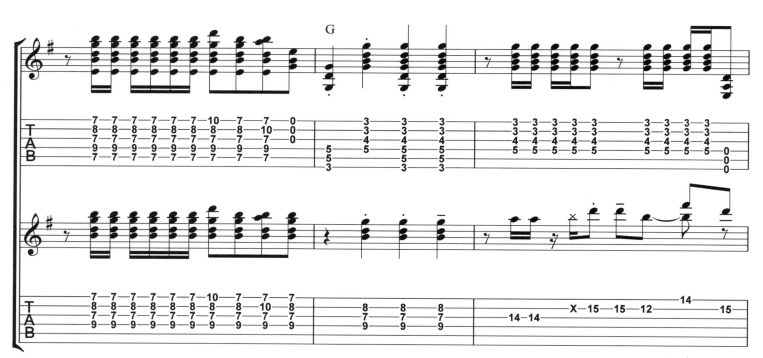

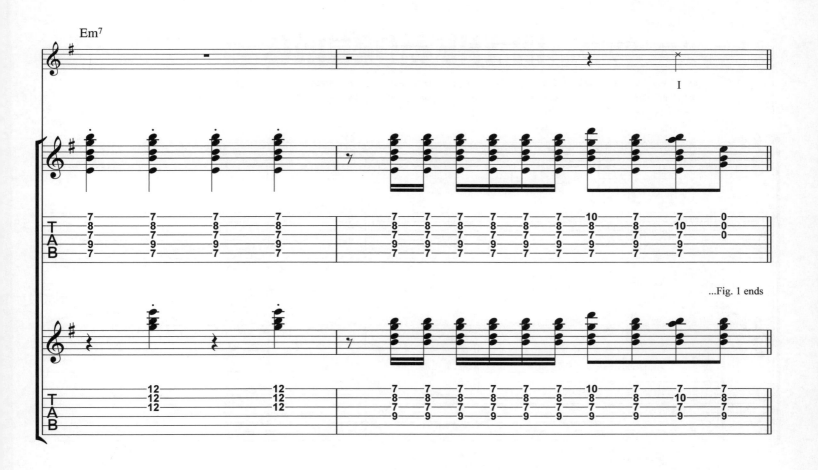

Verse

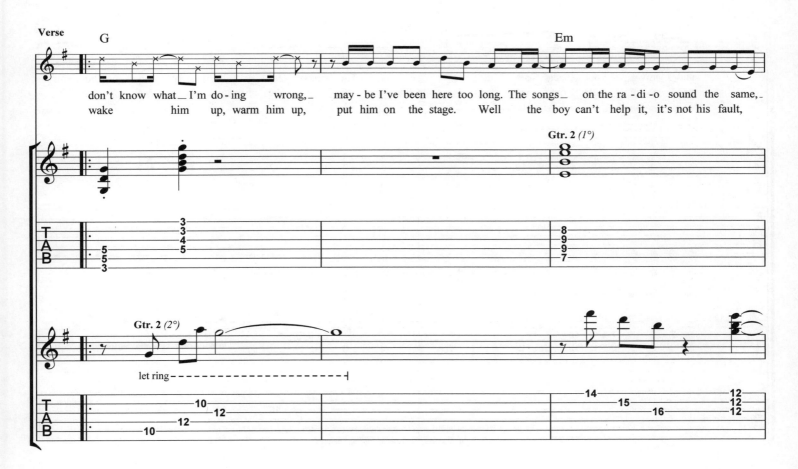

don't know what__ I'm do-ing   wrong,__   may-be I've been here too long. The songs__   on the ra-di-o sound the   same,__
wake   him   up, warm him up,   put him on the stage.   Well   the boy can't help it, it's not his fault,

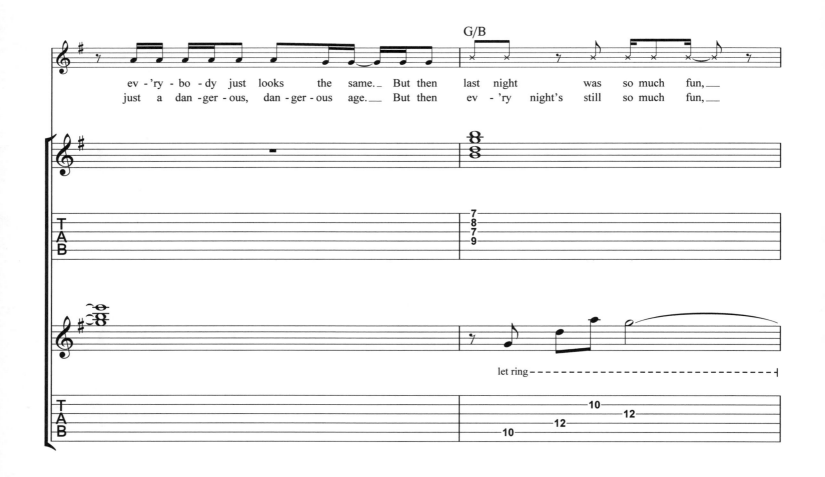

ev -'ry -bo -dy just looks the same._ But then last night was so much fun,_
just a dan -ger -ous, dan -ger -ous age._ But then ev -'ry night's still so much fun,_

let ring -|

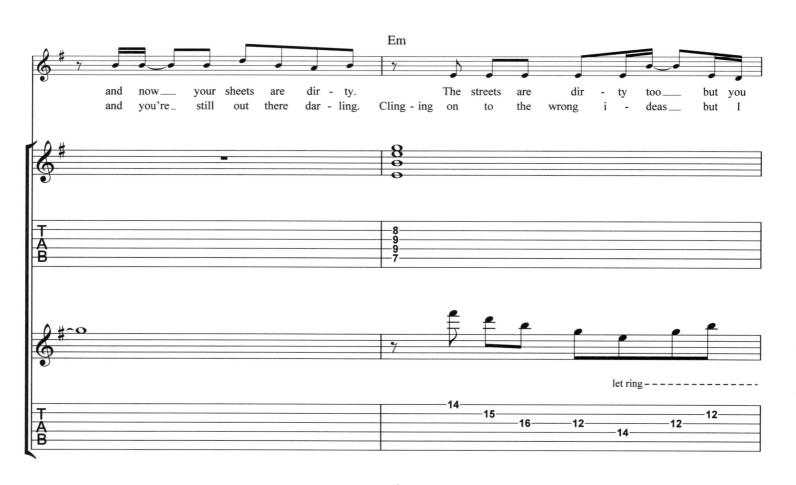

and now_ your sheets are dir - ty. The streets are dir - ty too_ but you
and you're_ still out there dar - ling. Cling -ing on to the wrong i - deas_ but I

let ring - - - - - - - - - - - - - - -

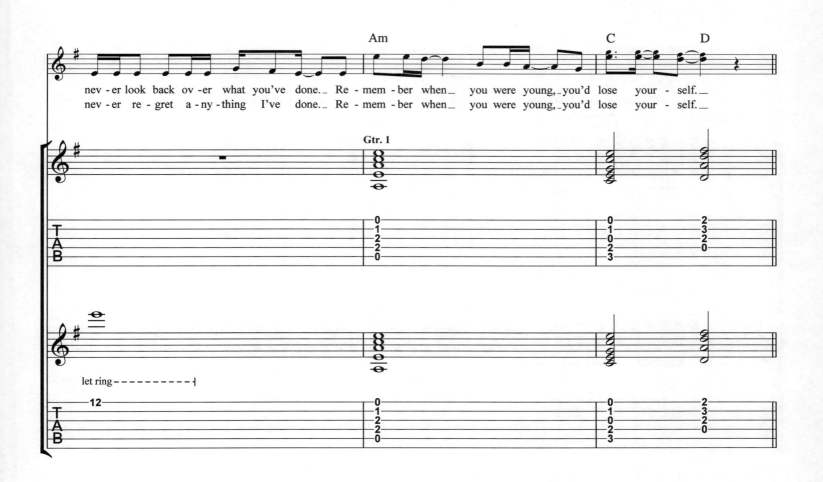

never look back over what you've done. Re-mem-ber when__ you were young, you'd lose__ your-self.__
never re-gret a-ny-thing I've done. Re-mem-ber when__ you were young, you'd lose__ your-self.__

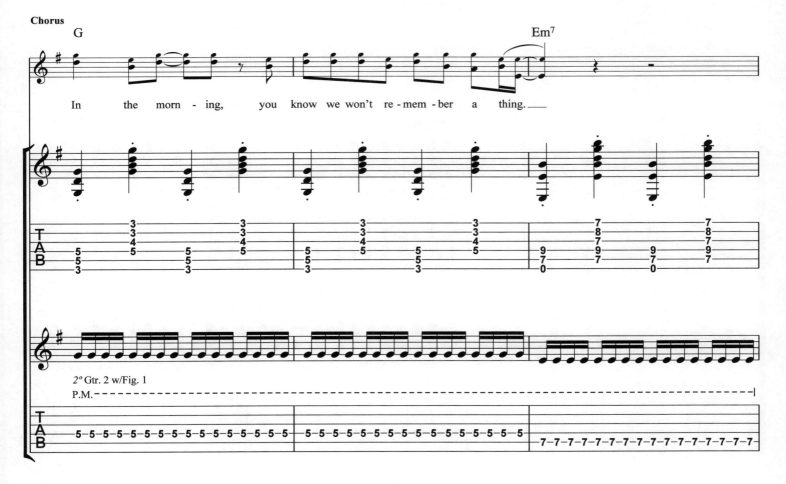

Chorus

In the morn-ing, you know we won't re-mem-ber a thing.__

2° Gtr. 2 w/Fig. 1
P.M.

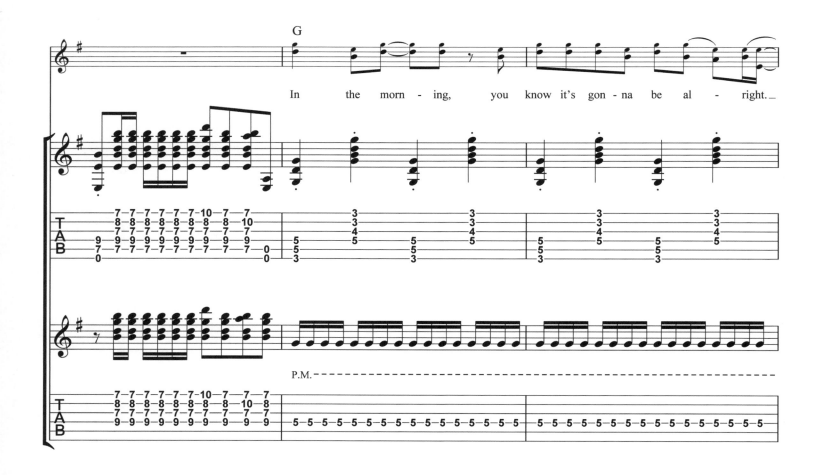

In the morn - ing,   you know it's gon - na be al - right.

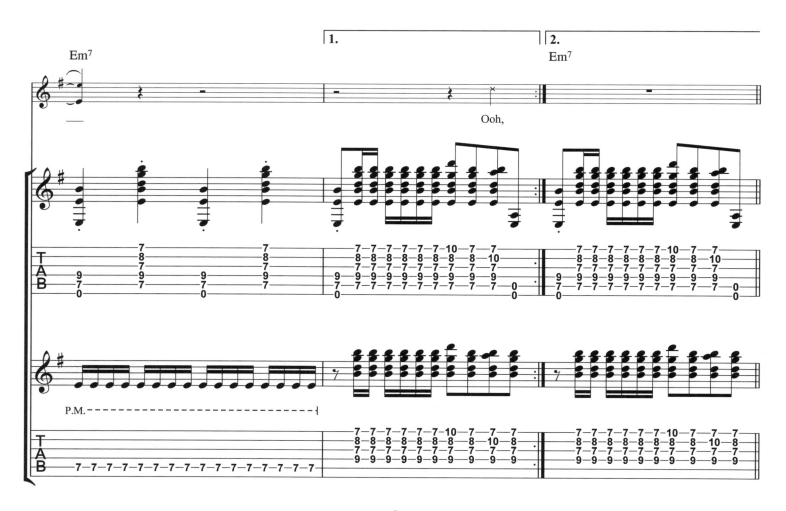

Ooh,

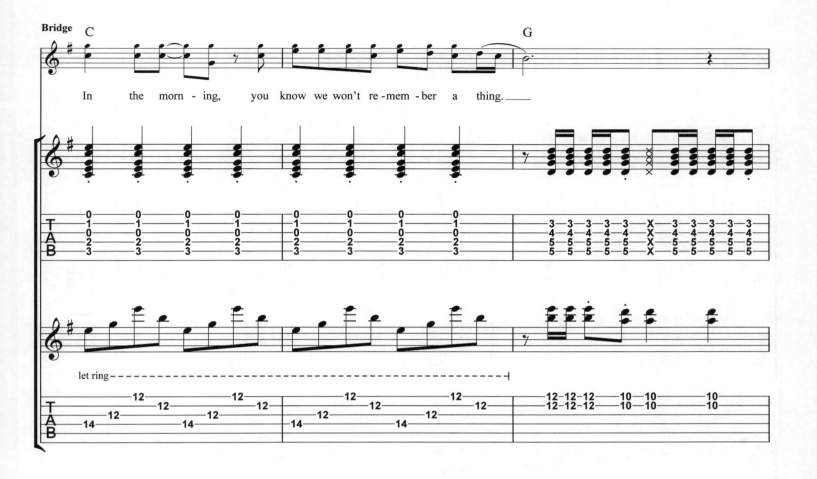

In the morn - ing, you know we won't re -mem - ber a thing.

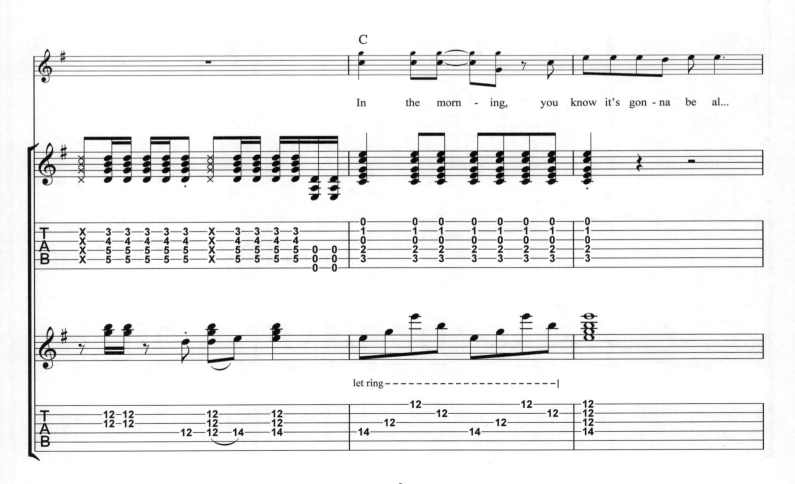

In the morn - ing, you know it's gon - na be al...

let ring

9

10

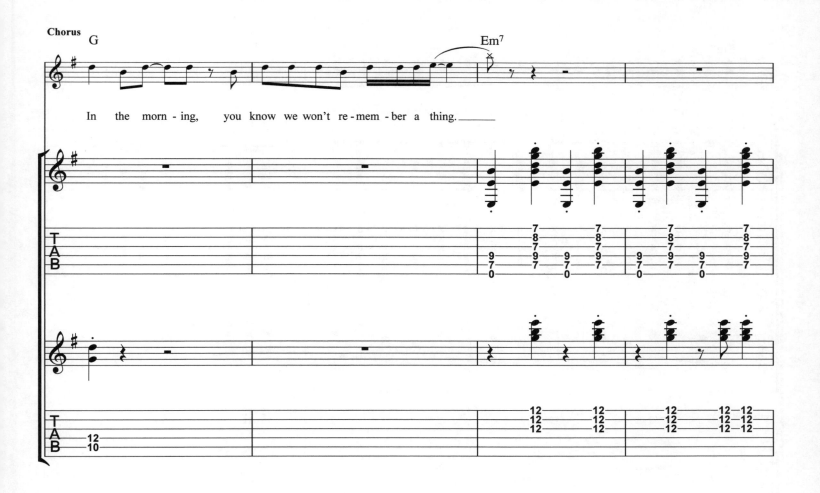

In the morn - ing, you know we won't re - mem - ber a thing.

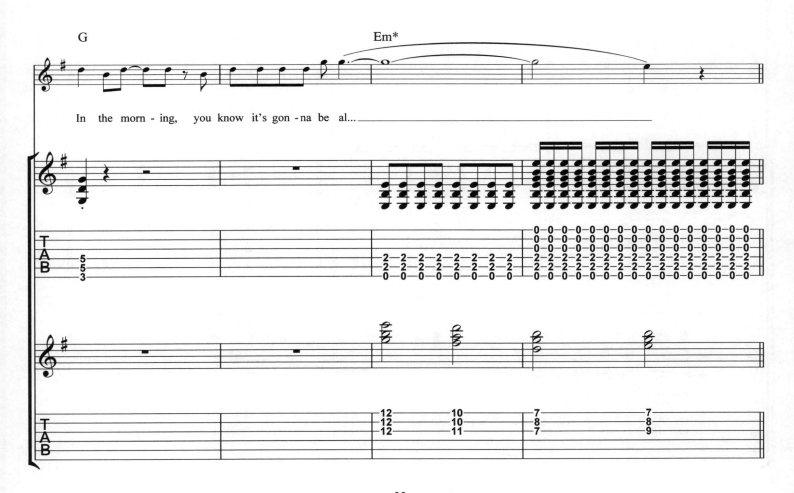

In the morn - ing, you know it's gon - na be al...

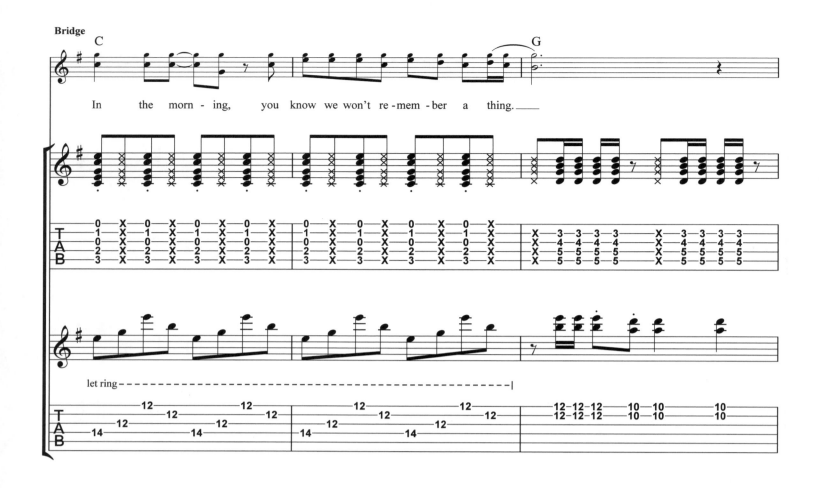

In the morn - ing, you know we won't re -mem - ber a thing. ___

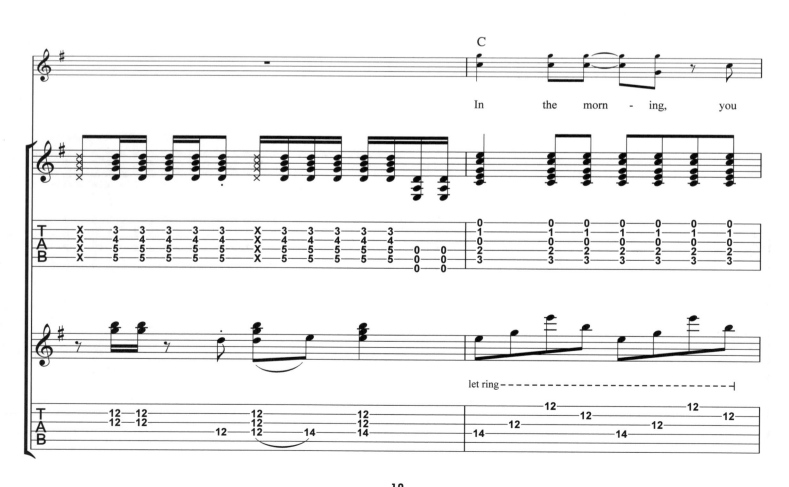

In the morn - ing, you

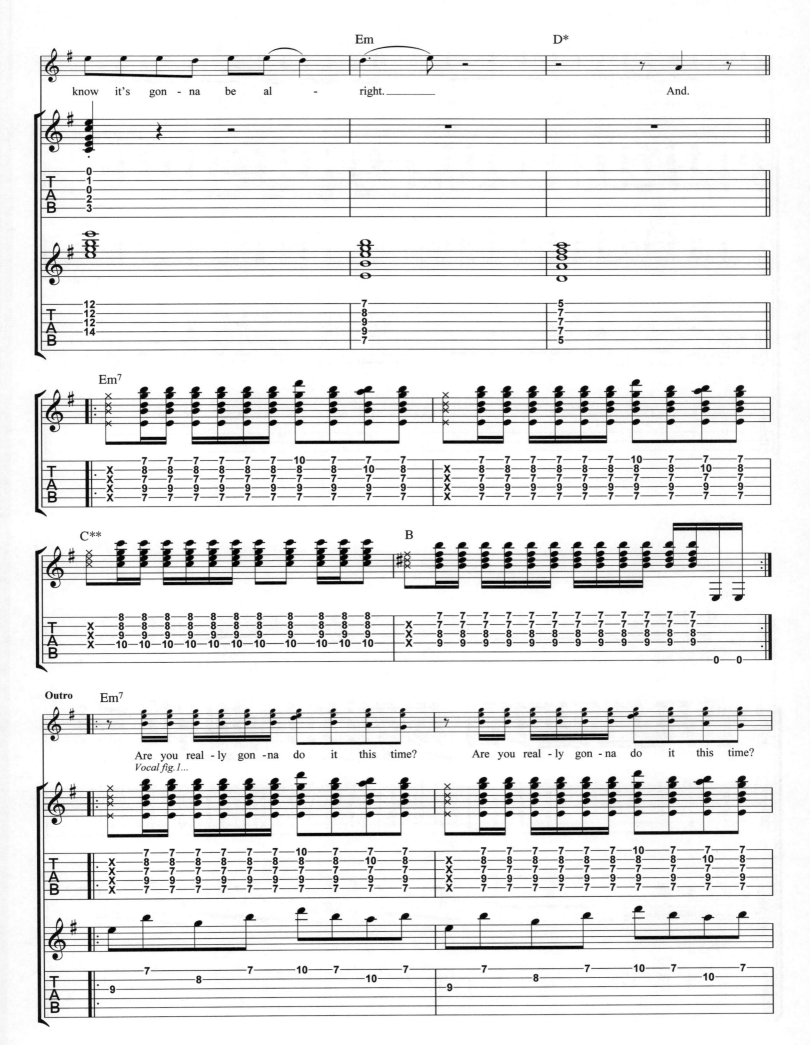

know it's gon - na be al - right. _____ And.

Em⁷

C**   B

Outro   Em⁷

Are you real - ly gon - na do it this time?   Are you real - ly gon - na do it this time?
Vocal fig.1...

13

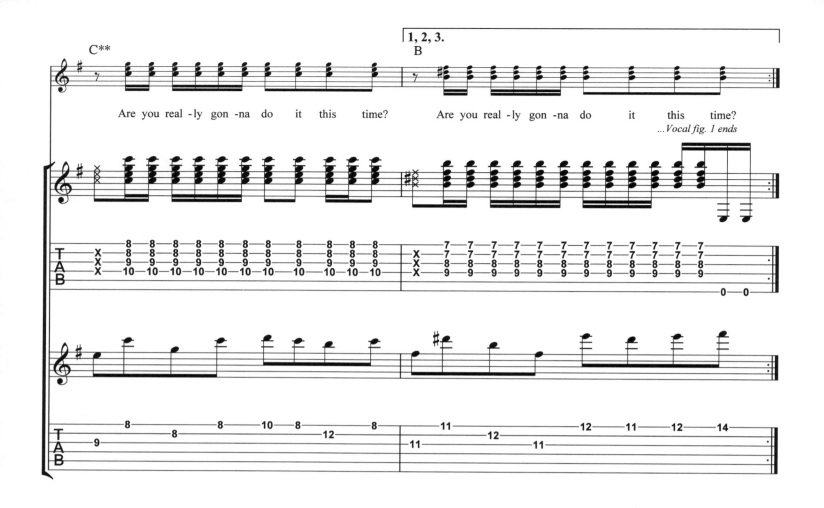

Are you real-ly gon-na do it this time? Are you real-ly gon-na do it this time?

...Vocal fig. 1 ends

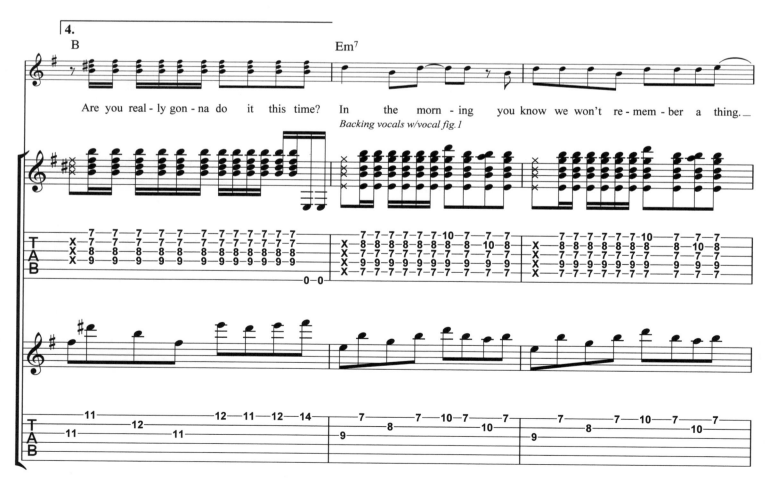

Are you real-ly gon-na do it this time? In the morn-ing you know we won't re-mem-ber a thing.

Backing vocals w/vocal fig.1

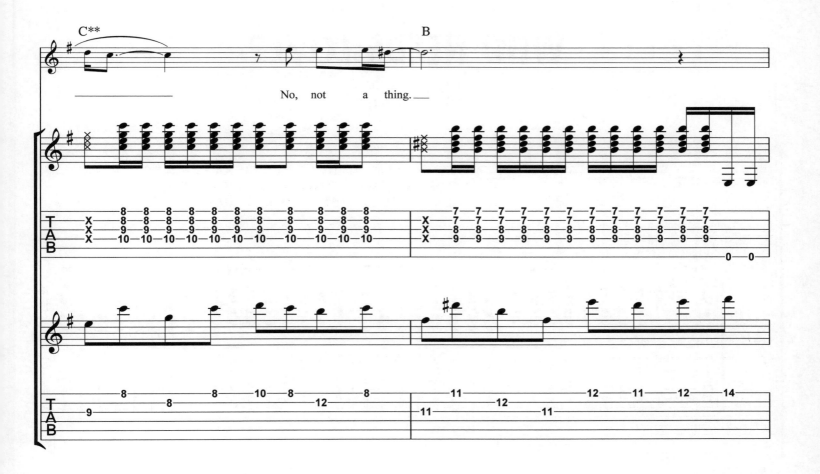

No, not a thing. ___

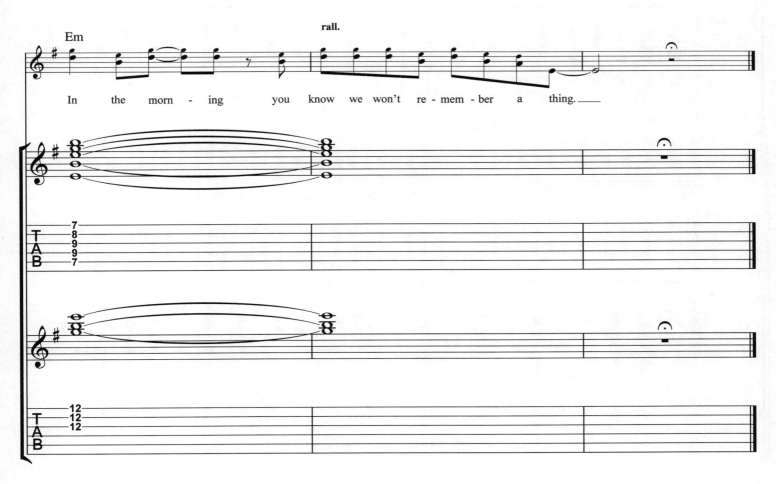

In the morn - ing   you know we won't re - mem - ber a thing. ___

WHO NEEDS LOVE?

Song by Johnny Borrell
Music by Razorlight

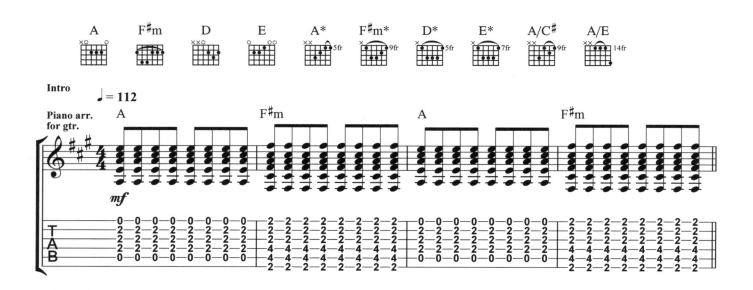

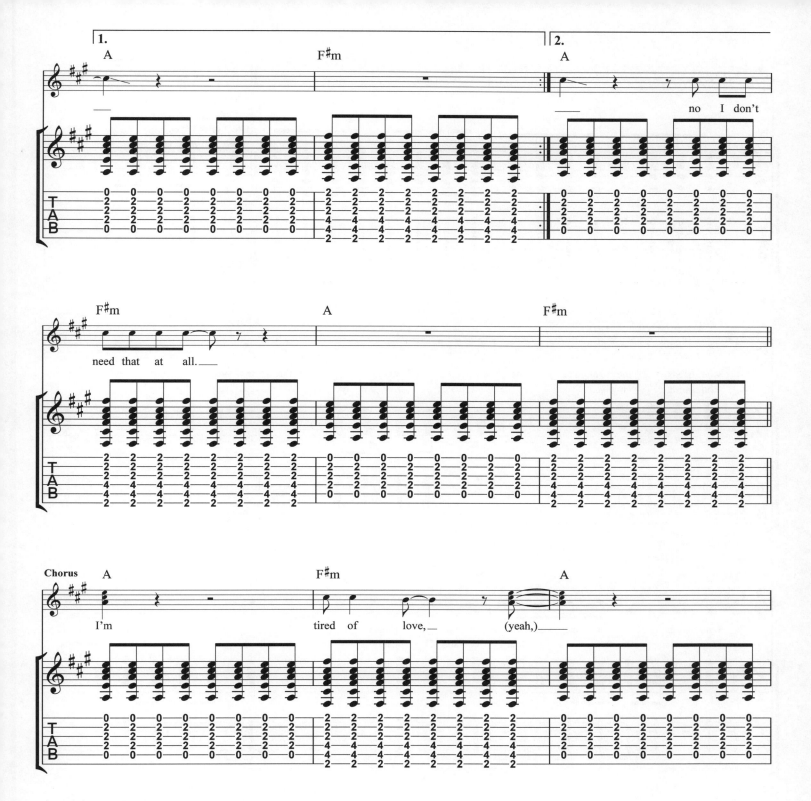

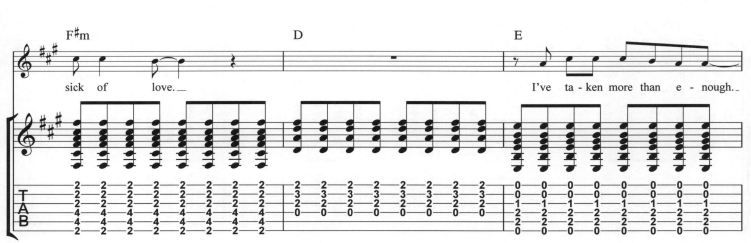

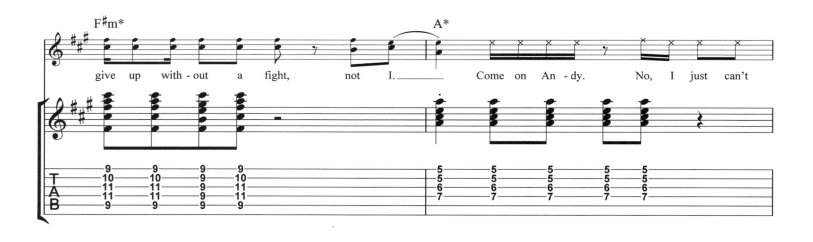

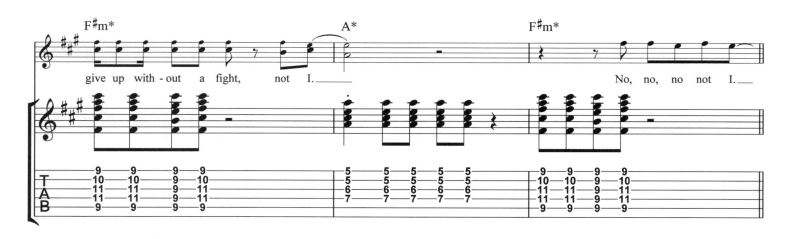

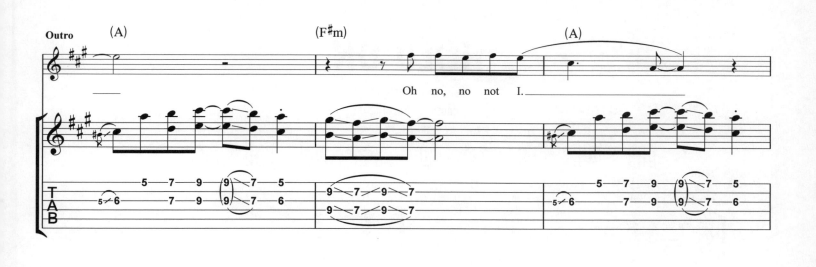

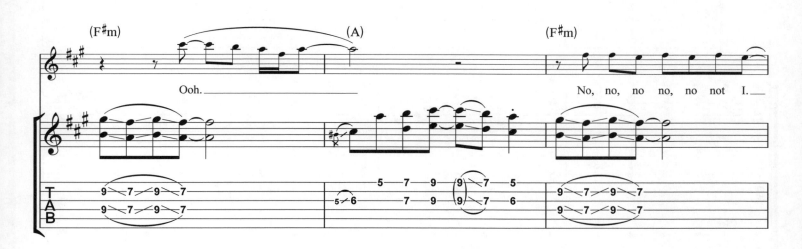

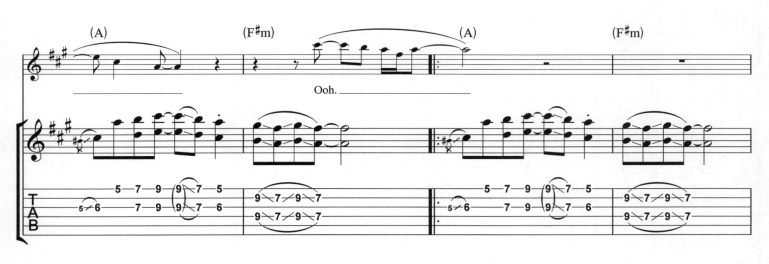

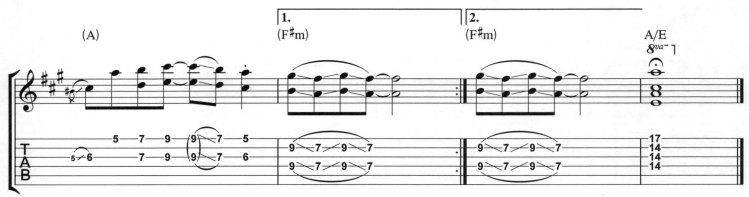

21

HOLD ON

Song by Johnny Borrell
Music by Razorlight

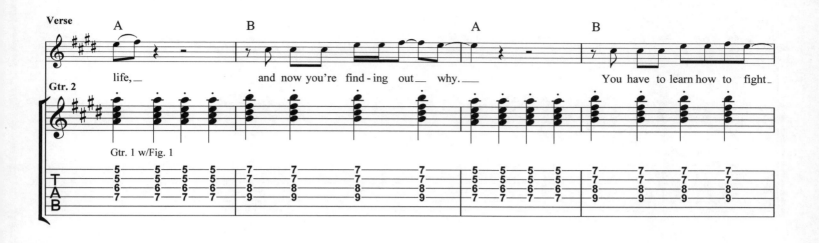

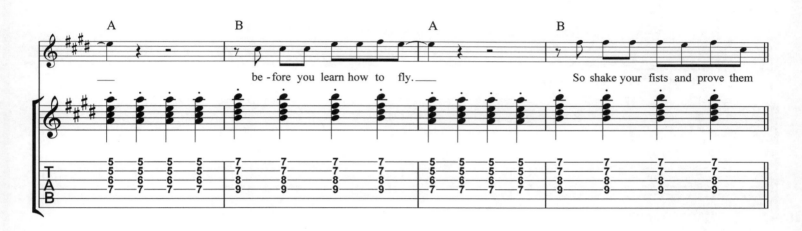

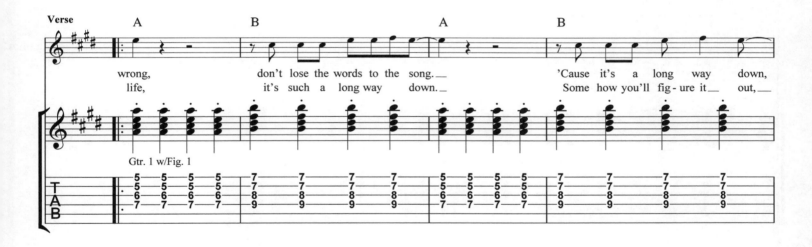

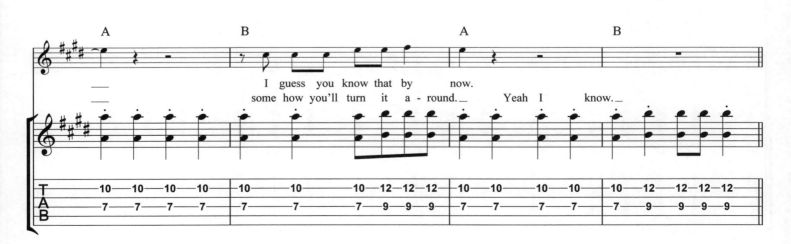

Chorus

And if you hold on,_____ well, I will hold on too.__

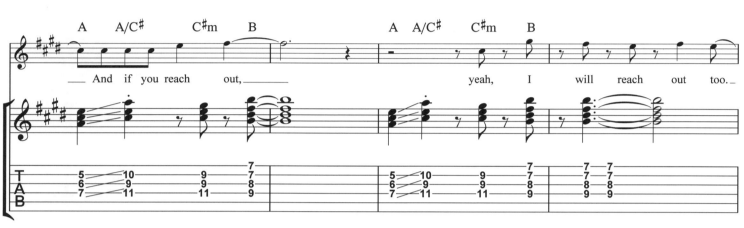

__ And if you reach out,_____ yeah, I will reach out too.

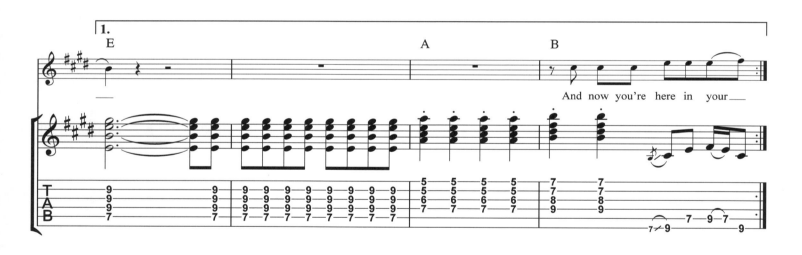

1.

And now you're here in your

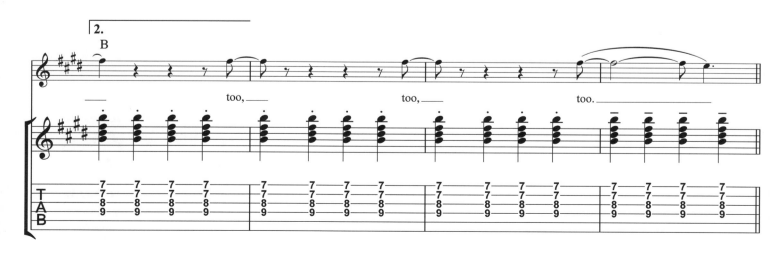

2.

__ too,_____ too,_____ too._____

AMERICA

Song by Johnny Borrell & Andy Burrows
Music by Razorlight

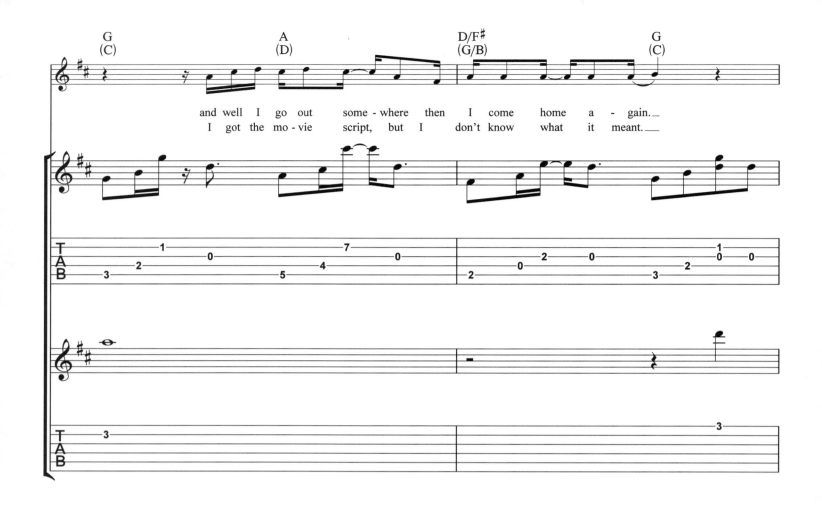

and well I go out some-where then I come home a - gain.____
I got the mo-vie script, but I don't know what it meant.____

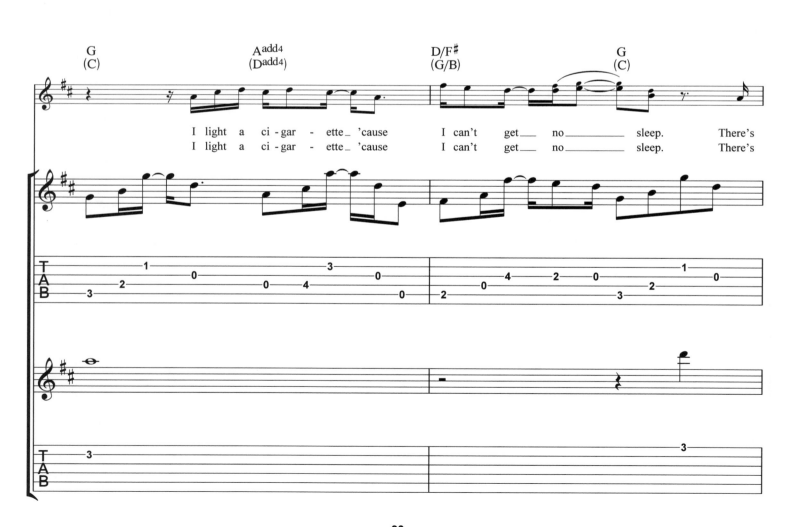

I light a ci-gar - ette_ 'cause I can't get__ no_____ sleep. There's
I light a ci-gar - ette_ 'cause I can't get__ no_____ sleep. There's

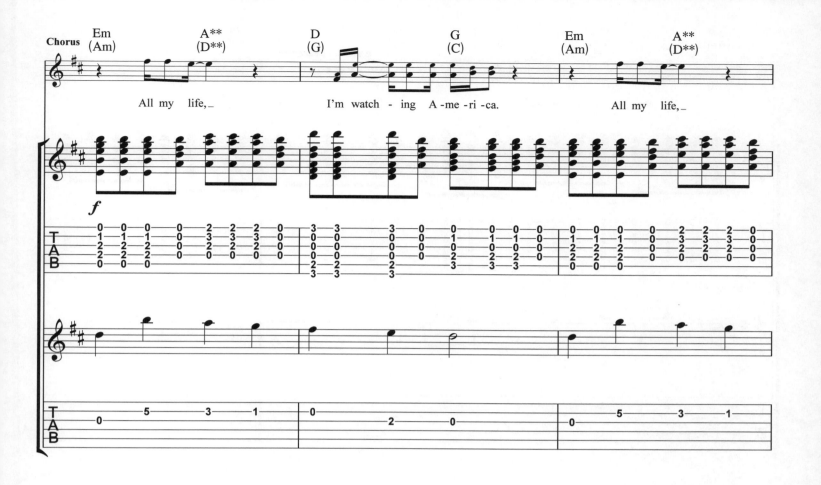

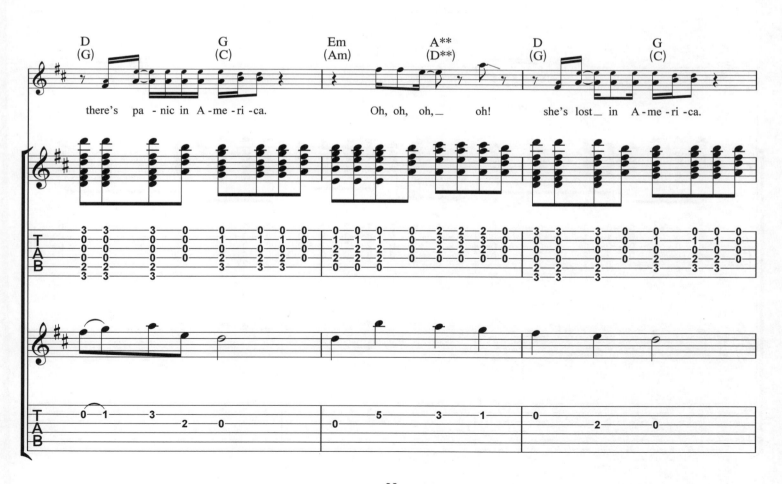

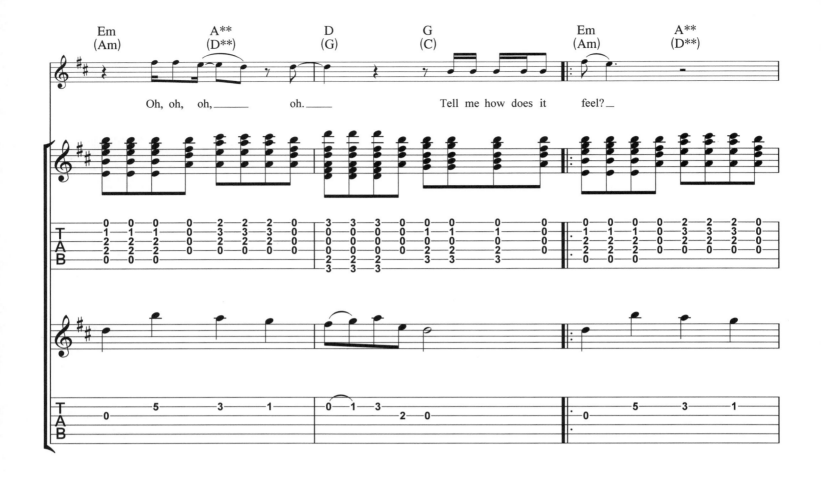

Oh, oh, oh, _____ oh. _____ Tell me how does it feel? _

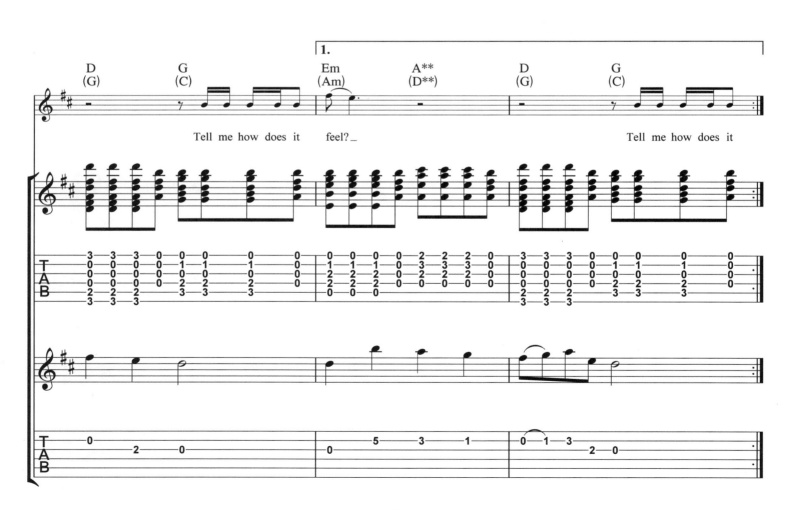

Tell me how does it feel? _ Tell me how does it

BEFORE I FALL TO PIECES

Song by Johnny Borrell & Andy Burrows
Music by Razorlight

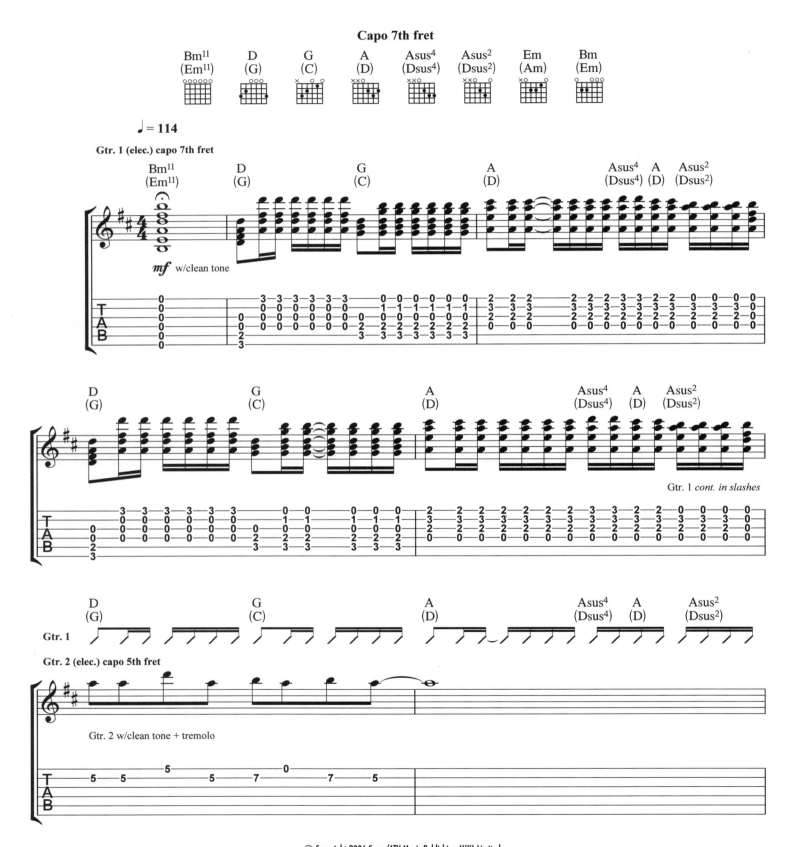

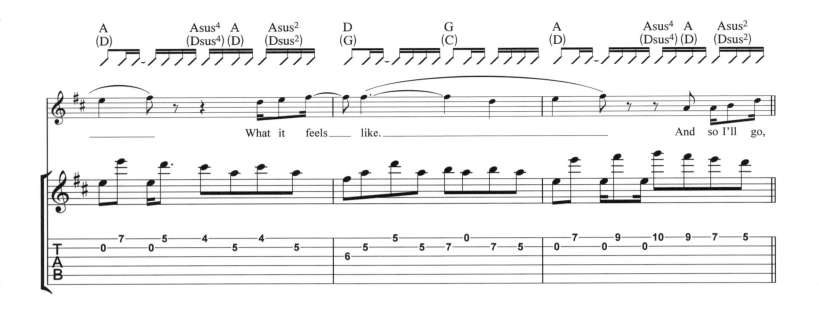

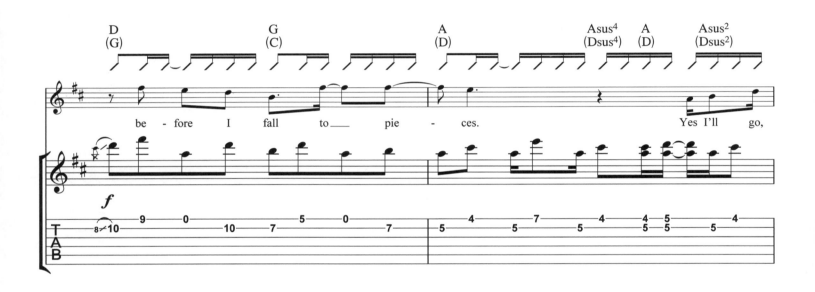

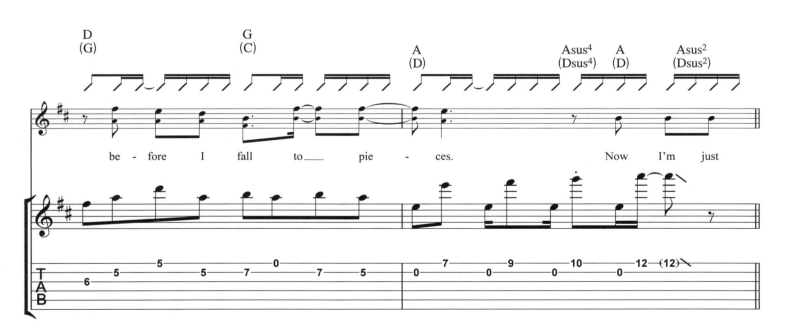

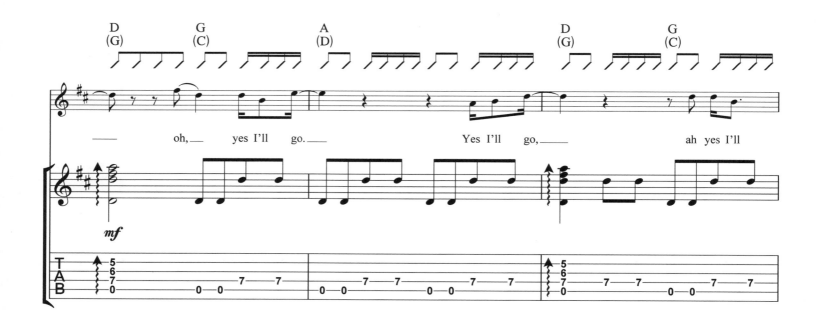

oh,___ yes I'll go.___ Yes I'll go,___ ah yes I'll

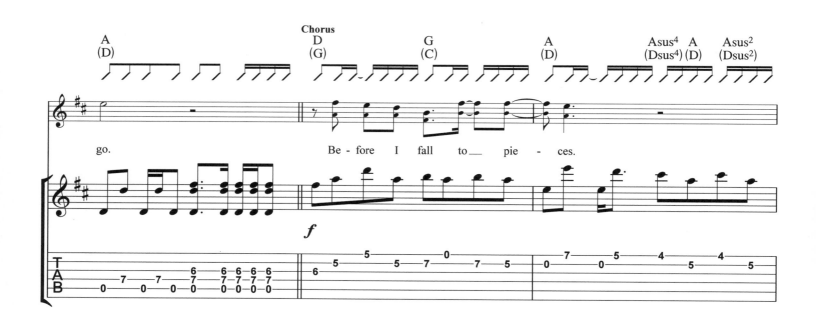

go. Be - fore I fall to___ pie - ces.

Be - fore I fall to___ pie - ces. Yes I'll go, be - fore I fall to___ pie -

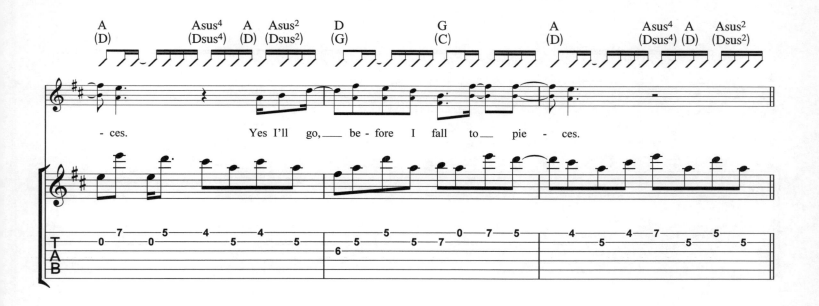

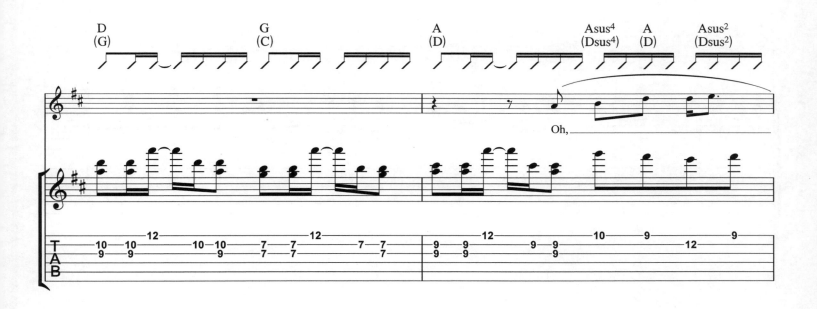

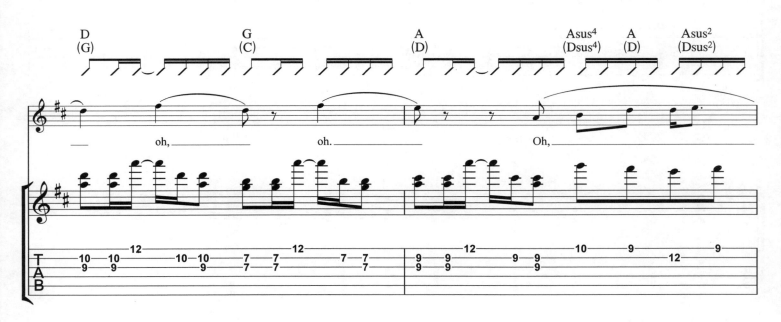

I CAN'T STOP THIS FEELING I'VE GOT

Song by Johnny Borrell & Björn Ågren
Music by Razorlight

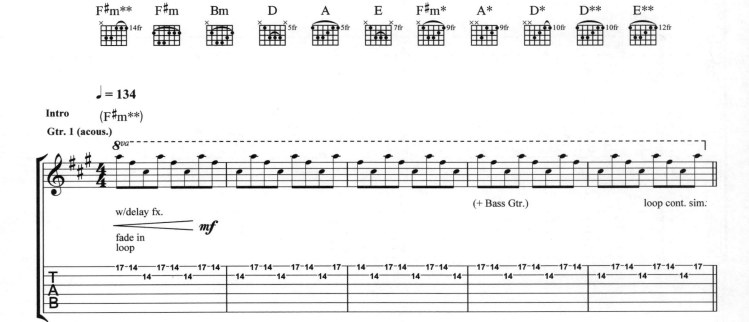

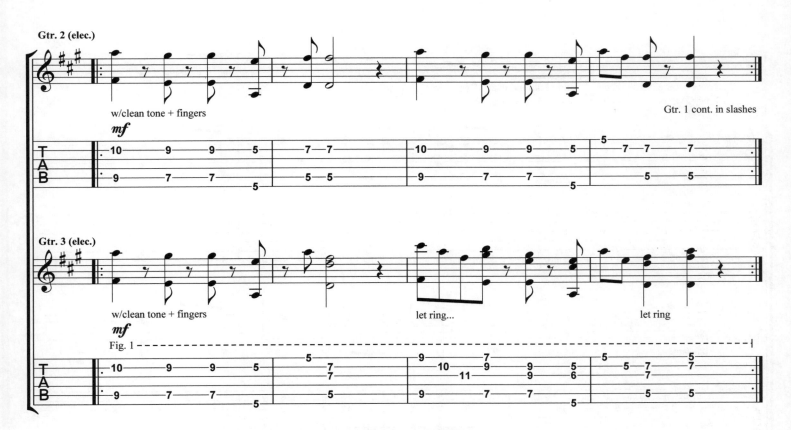

Verse

1, 2, %. I___ can't_ stop this feel-ing I've_ got, I know who I___ am___ and I know what I am_ not.   1°, % {I
                                                                                                      2° {I

know where I've_ been___ and I know what I've_ lost,─ } but I_____ can't_ stop this feel-ing I've_ got.
know what I've_ gained_ and I know what I've_ lost,_ }   % The

* cancel delay fx.

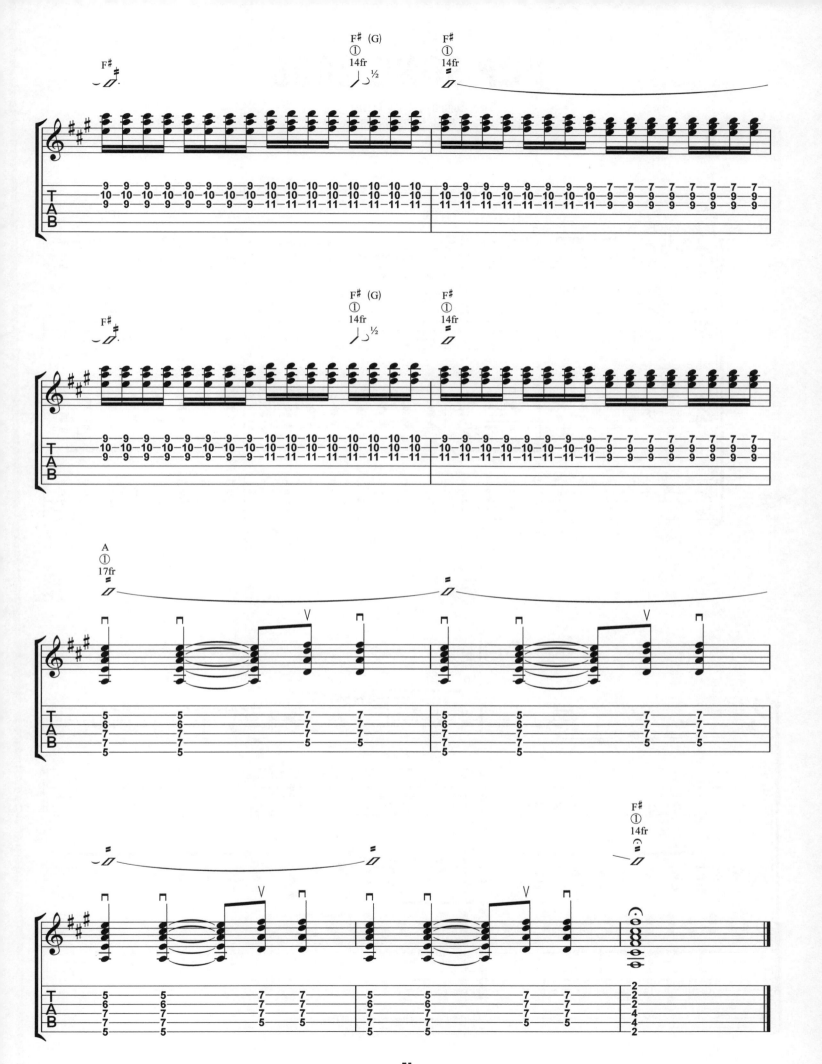

POP SONG 2006

Song by Johnny Borrell
Music by Razorlight

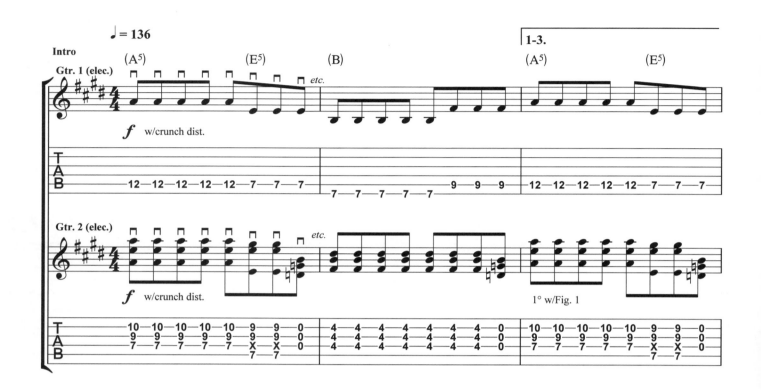

Verse

1. Ev - 'ry - one   is   los - in' it,   ev - 'ry - bo - dy's   giv - in'   up.
2. Some - how   ea - sy   but   she   is   hard   to   touch

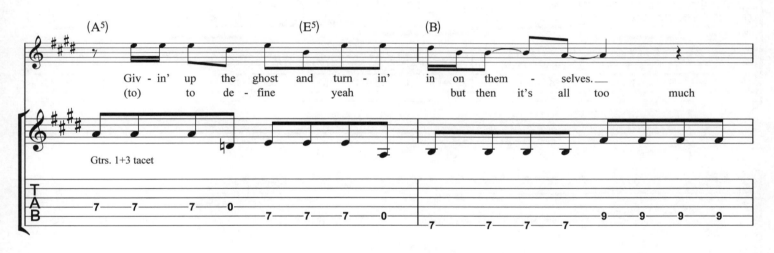

Giv - in' up   the   ghost   and   turn - in'   in   on   them - selves. ___
(to)   to   de - fine   yeah   but   then   it's   all   too   much

Gtrs. 1+3 tacet

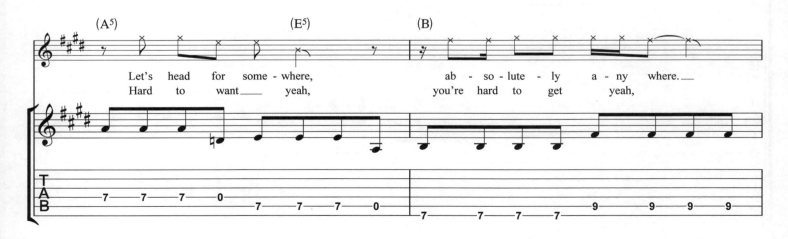

Let's   head   for   some - where,   ab - so - lute - ly   a - ny   where. ___
Hard   to   want ___   yeah,   you're   hard   to   get   yeah,

53

* Combined part.

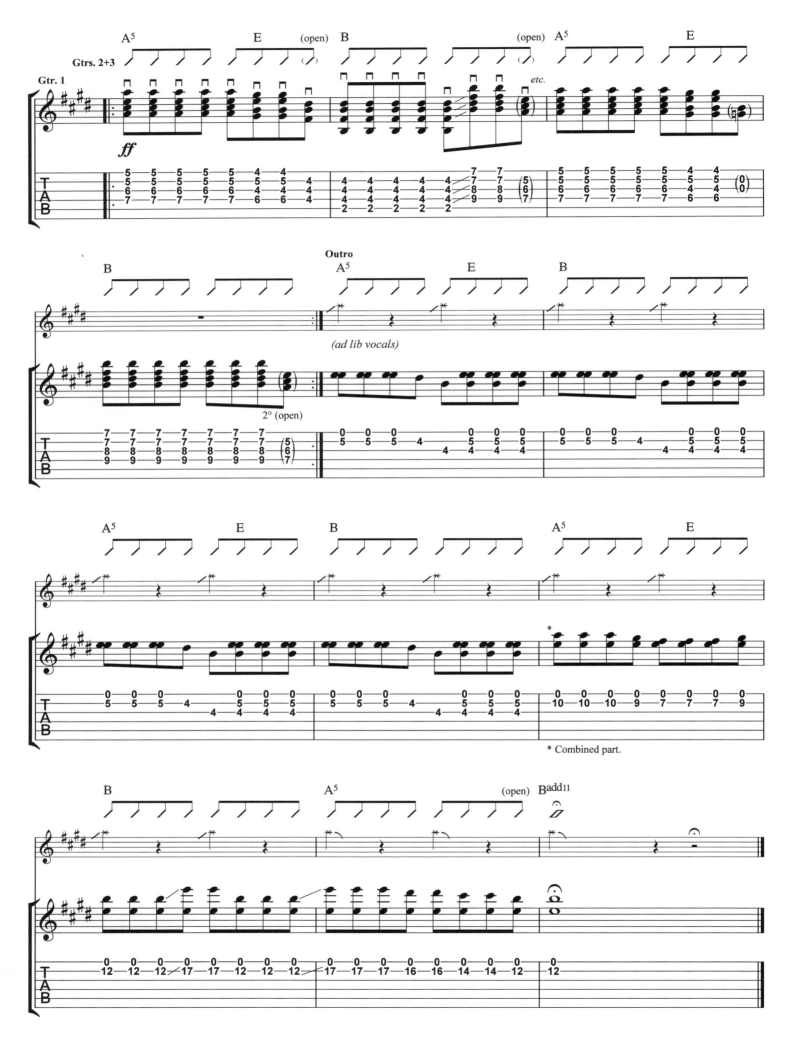

KIRBY'S HOUSE

Song by Johnny Borrell
Music by Razorlight

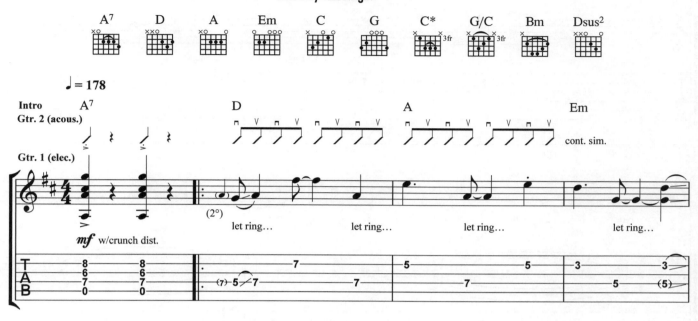

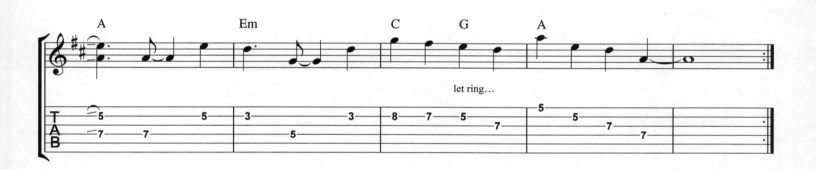

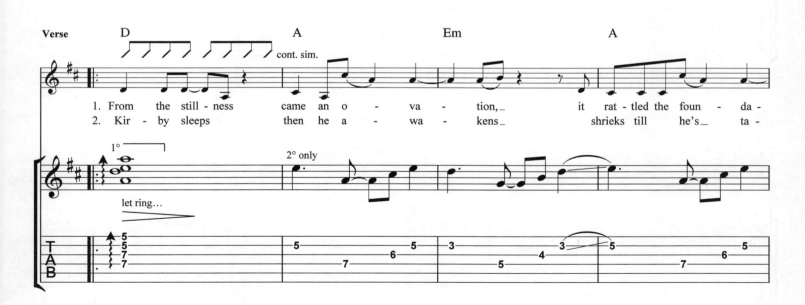

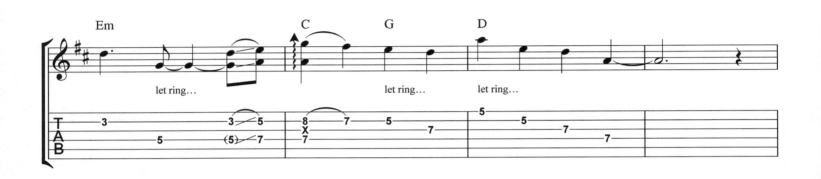

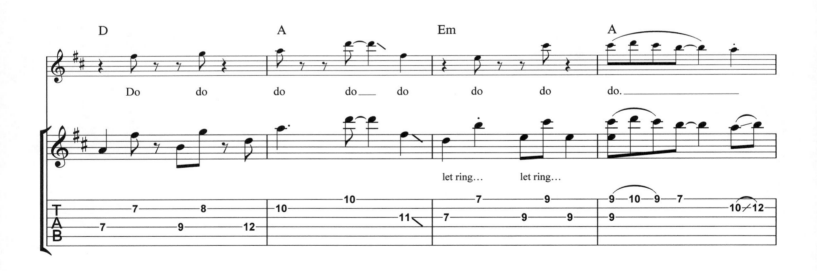

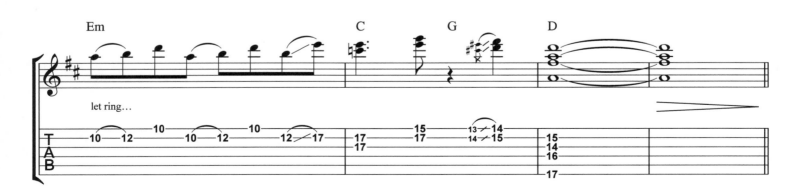

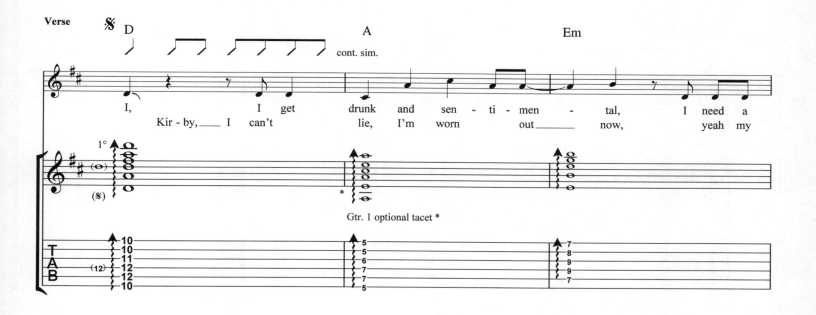

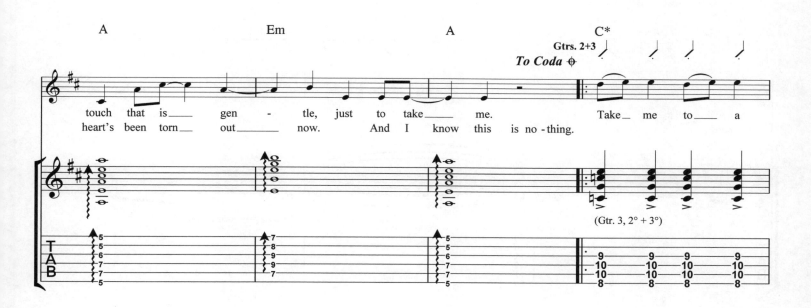

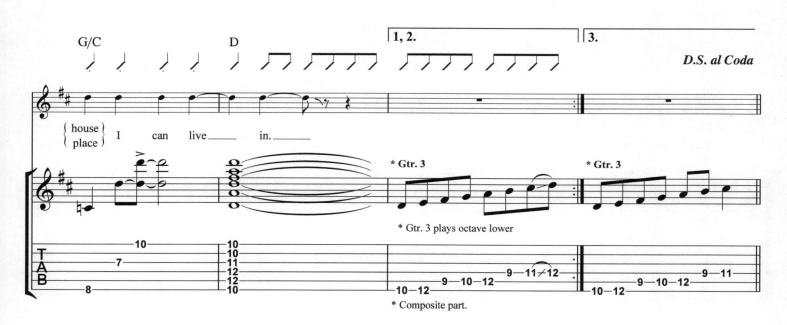

63

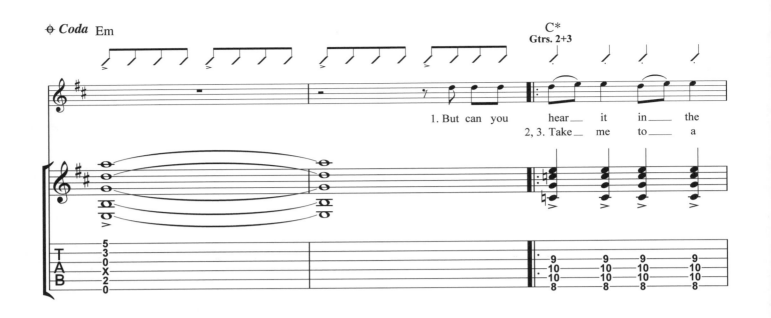

1. But can you hear__ it in__ the
2, 3. Take__ me to__ a

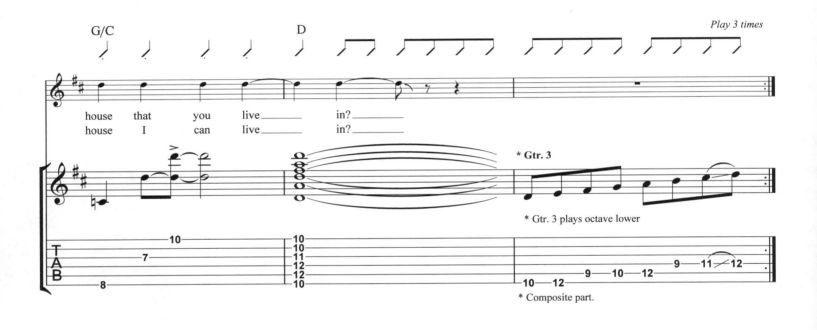

house that you live_____ in?_____
house I you can live_____ in?_____

* Gtr. 3 plays octave lower

* Composite part.

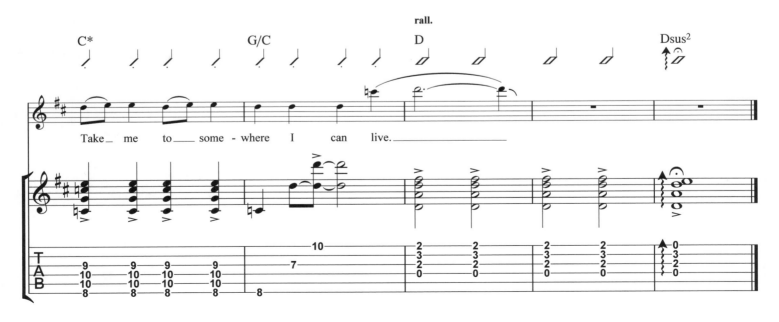

Take__ me to_____ some - where I can live.___

64

BACK TO THE START

Song by Johnny Borrell
Music by Razorlight

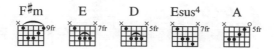

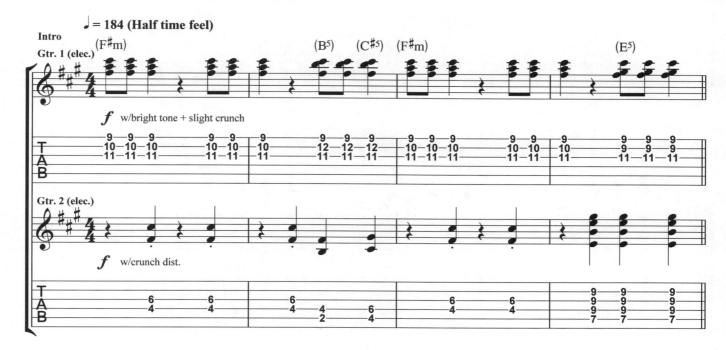

66

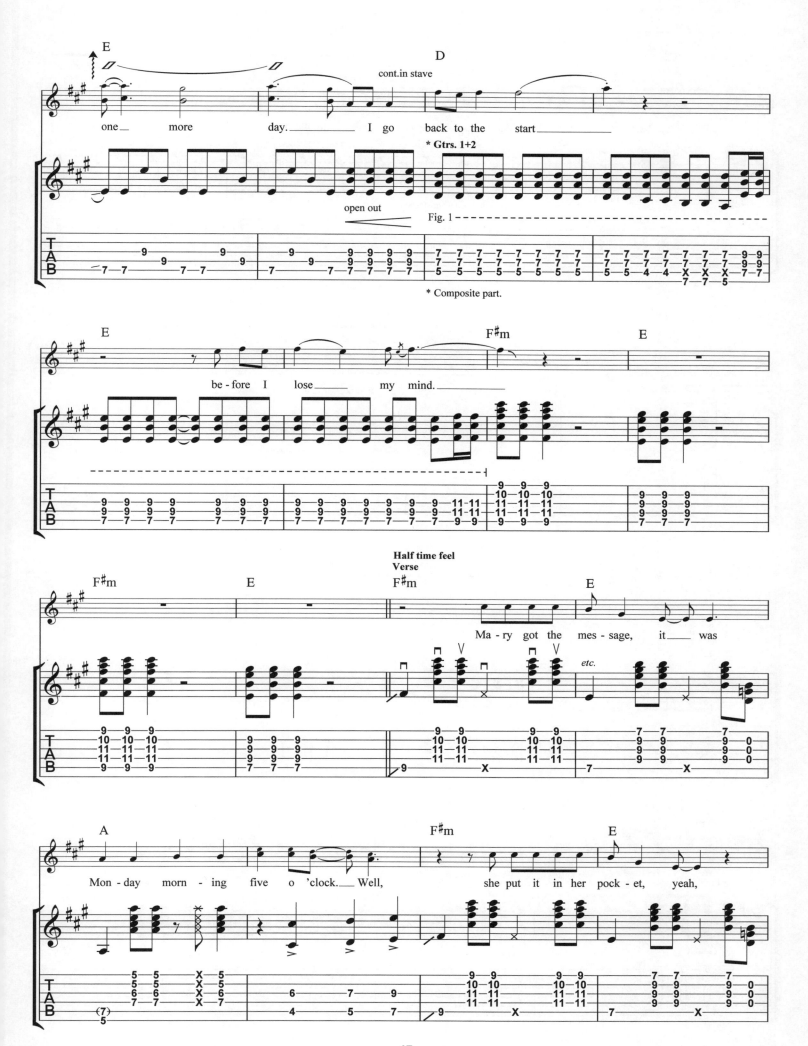

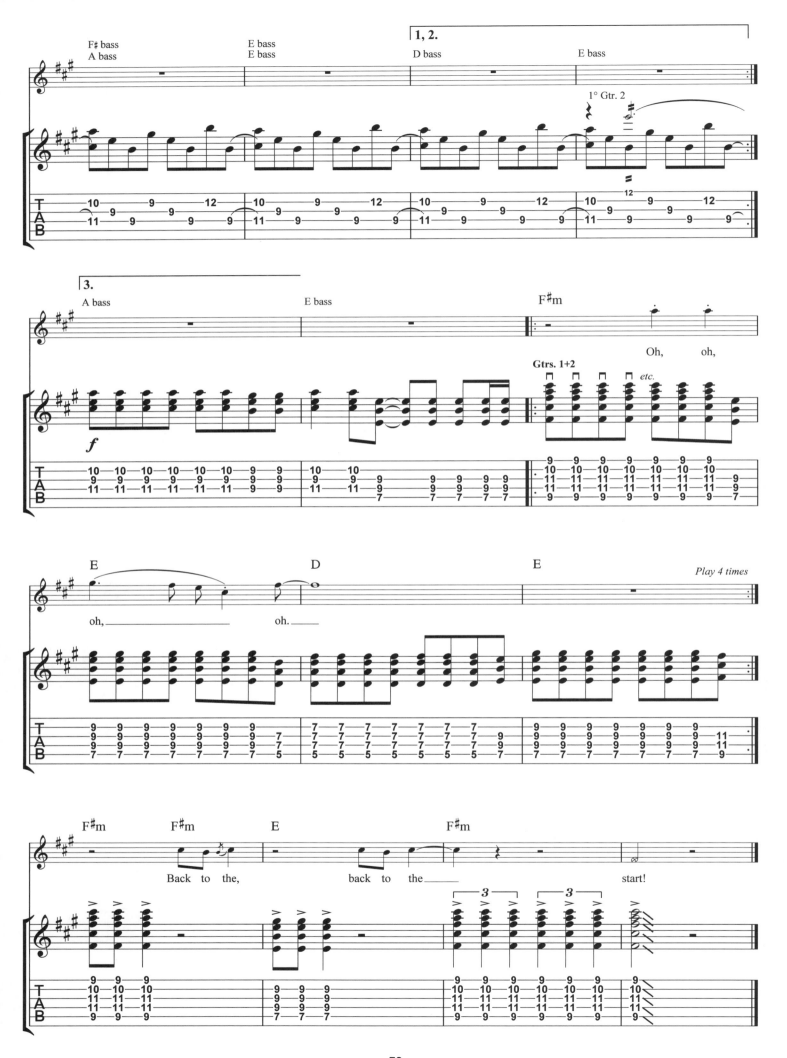

LOS ANGELES WALTZ

Song by Johnny Borrell
Music by Razorlight

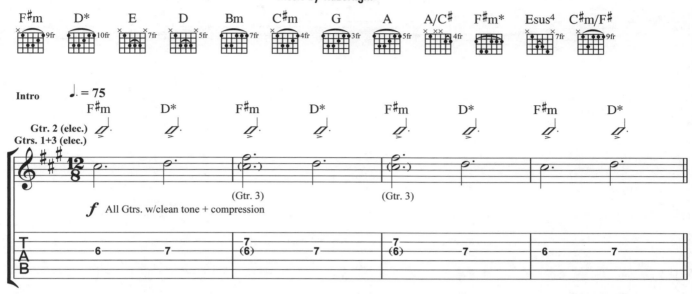

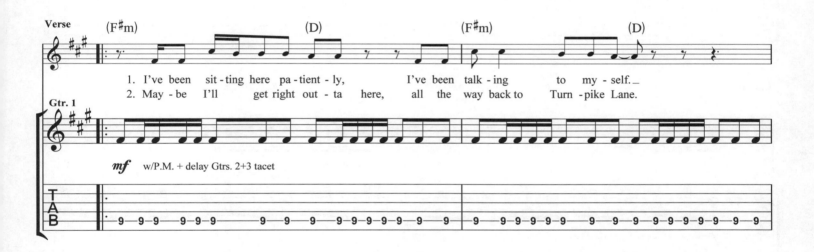

1. I've been sit-ting here pa-tient-ly, I've been talk-ing to my-self.
2. May-be I'll get right out-ta here, all the way back to Turn-pike Lane.

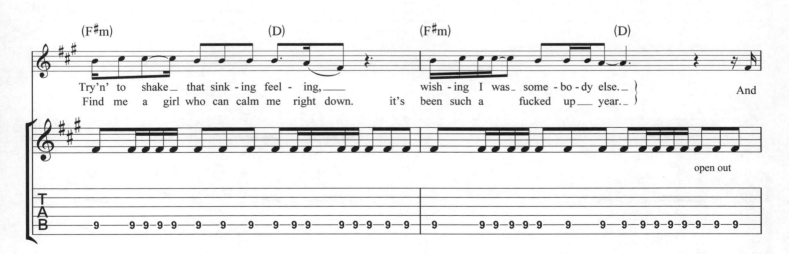

Try'n' to shake that sink-ing feel-ing, wish-ing I was some-bo-dy else. And
Find me a girl who can calm me right down. it's been such a fucked up year.

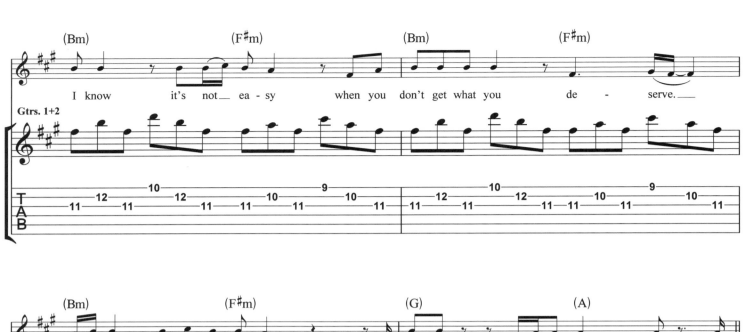

I know it's not ea - sy when you don't get what you de - serve.

Gtrs. 1+2

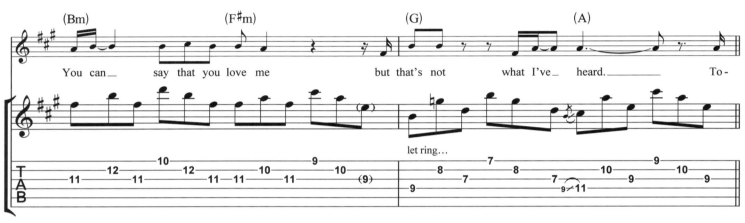

You can say that you love me but that's not what I've heard. To-

let ring...

Chorus

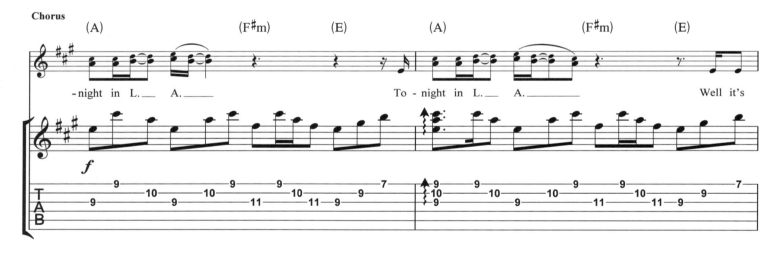

-night in L. A. To - night in L. A. Well it's

1.

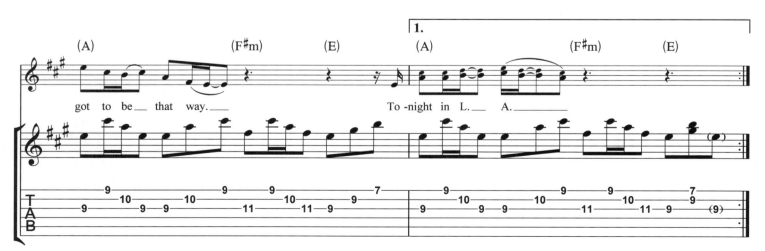

got to be that way. To -night in L. A.

Guitar Tablature Explained

Guitar music can be notated in three different ways: on a musical stave, in tablature, and in rhythm slashes

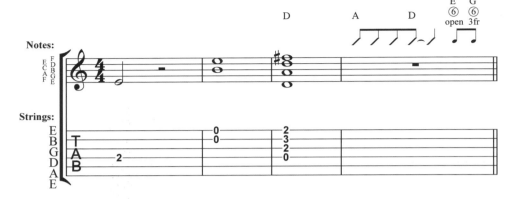

RHYTHM SLASHES: are written above the stave. Strum chords in the rhythm indicated. Round noteheads indicate single notes.

THE MUSICAL STAVE: shows pitches and rhythms and is divided by lines into bars. Pitches are named after the first seven letters of the alphabet.

TABLATURE: graphically represents the guitar fingerboard. Each horizontal line represents a string, and each number represents a fret.

Definitions for special guitar notation

SEMI-TONE BEND: Strike the note and bend up a semi-tone (½ step).

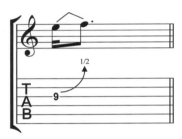

WHOLE-TONE BEND: Strike the note and bend up a whole-tone (full step).

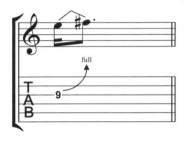

GRACE NOTE BEND: Strike the note and bend as indicated. Play the first note as quickly as possible.

QUARTER-TONE BEND: Strike the note and bend up a ¼ step

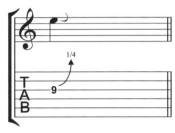

BEND & RELEASE: Strike the note and bend up as indicated, then release back to the original note.

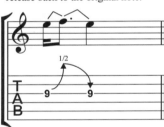

COMPOUND BEND & RELEASE: Strike the note and bend up and down in the rhythm indicated.

PRE-BEND: Bend the note as indicated, then strike it.

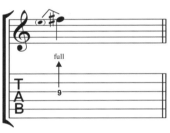

PRE-BEND & RELEASE: Bend the note as indicated. Strike it and release the note back to the original pitch.

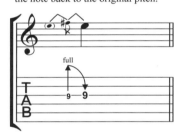

HAMMER-ON: Strike the first note with one finger, then sound the second note (on the same string) with another finger by fretting it without picking.

PULL-OFF: Place both fingers on the note to be sounded, strike the first note and without picking, pull the finger off to sound the second note.

LEGATO SLIDE (GLISS): Strike the first note and then slide the same fret-hand finger up or down to the second note. The second note is not struck.

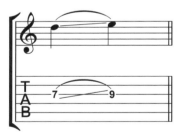

MUFFLED STRINGS: A percussive sound is produced by laying the first hand across the string(s) without depressing, and striking them with the pick hand.

NATURAL HARMONIC: Strike the note while the fret-hand lightly touches the string directly over the fret indicated.

PICK SCRAPE: The edge of the pick is rubbed down (or up) the string, producing a scratchy sound.

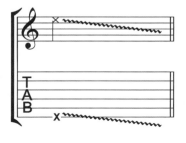

PALM MUTING: The note is partially muted by the pick hand lightly touching the string(s) just before the bridge.

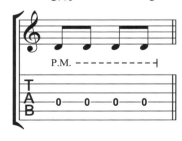

SHIFT SLIDE (GLISS & RESTRIKE) Same as legato slide, except the second note is struck.

1 2 3 4 5 6 7 8 9